D0410946

Gulls in Britain

Several species of our gulls on the foreshore at
Bridlington in winter.

Gulls in Britain

By

Richard Vaughan

H. F. & G. WITHERBY LTD

First published in 1972 by
H F & G WITHERBY LTD
15 Nicholas Lane, London, EC4

© Richard Vaughan 1972

SBN 85493 309 7

Printed photolitho in Great Britain by
Ebenezer Baylis and Son Limited
The Trinity Press, Worcester, and London

Contents

Introduction

In almost every part of the world the so-called seagull has become a familiar and generally much-loved bird. Familiar because it haunts not the open sea but the coasts, the countryside cultivated by man, and his towns and cities too. Much-loved no doubt because of its graceful flight, melodious cry and beautiful grey and white plumage. Of the forty-three different species of gull generally recognised by ornithologists, twenty-nine breed in the Northern Hemisphere. Six of these are common British breeding birds. A further dozen or so species of gull have been identified here but most of them are extremely rare vagrants, apart from the little gull (*Larus minutus*), which appears regularly and in some areas in considerable numbers, especially on autumn passage, and the glaucous gull (*Larus hyperboreus*), which is a regular winter visitor in small numbers to the east coast especially. But this book is primarily concerned with the six common British gulls.

Although all adult gulls have predominantly grey and white plumage, their young are mostly speckled brown, and this may have been true of the remote ancestor of the gulls. They are thought to be white underneath because this makes it harder for a fish to see them when diving down to attack, while their black and white wing-tip patterns perhaps play a role in species recognition by the birds themselves. In all gulls the plumage of the sexes is identical, but males are usually slightly larger than females. Most species are gregarious, breeding colonially on the ground, sometimes on cliffs, and forming large flocks in winter for purposes of feeding and roosting. The only transequatorial migrant among gulls is Franklin's gull, but most European species undertake southerly movements in winter.

In spite of the difficulties in counting them, gulls have been conclusively shown to be increasing more or less rapidly in numbers, encouraged no doubt by the protection now afforded them in most European countries and by supplies of food, notably in refuse tips and at fish docks, liberally provided for them by man. In some areas, especially in nature reserves, they have become so numerous as to prejudice the successful breeding of other birds, rarer and more interesting than they. Thus at Havergate in Suffolk the Royal Society for the Protection of Birds has had to limit drastically the numbers of breeding black-headed gulls in order to protect the avocets, and a sustained programme of destruction of the larger gulls and their eggs has been carried out on Skomer Island, Pembrokeshire, a National Nature Reserve, in the hope of improving thereby the breeding success and numbers of other sea-birds. Can gulls be regarded as pests? The case against them as presented in a recent symposium entitled "Gulls as Pests" is a poor one. Indeed, the group of ornithologists who contributed to the discussion could find no significant quantitative evidence against the gulls. Instead, they were accused of spoiling two square miles of grouse-shooting in Lancashire by breeding all over the moor, of preying on poultry, and even of spreading disease. In fact, it is clear that gulls are agriculturally beneficial and, even in places like Whitby and Dover, where they nest on houses and foul pavements and roofs, most people regard them with pleasure, rather than as a nuisance.

I gratefully place on record here my debt to my wife and children, who so often helped me to obtain the illustrations for this book, and to Mr H. N. Southern, who first taught me how to photograph birds. I would also like to thank all those ornithologists who so readily and helpfully replied to my letters of enquiry about gulls; Mr Antony Witherby for making this book better than it would otherwise have been; and Mr James Ferguson-Lees for numerous valuable emendations.

January 1972   RICHARD VAUGHAN

The Black-headed Gull *Larus ridibundus*

The chocolate-brown hood of the black-headed gull, together with its dark red legs and bill, only serve to distinguish it from other British gulls between March and July. In winter its small size, whiter appearance, and yellowish-red legs and bill, as well as the black spot behind the eye, are its principal field marks. In many areas, and at most times of year, it is our commonest gull inland. During this century it has considerably extended its breeding range in Europe, colonising Norway in 1880, Iceland in 1911, and Spain in the 1960's. In the British Isles it nests in large and small colonies on shingle beaches, among sand dunes, in salt-marshes, on islands in hill lochs, on moors and marshes, and in flooded gravel pits. The largest colony at the moment is probably that at Needs Oar Point in Hampshire,

9

which is thought to have increased from 1,200 pairs in 1962 to about 20,000 pairs in 1971. Running it a close second is the famous Ravenglass gullery in Cumberland, where the birds nest on dunes among a luxuriant growth of nettles, burdock and other plants caused by their accumulated droppings. Here the nests have in recent years been very carefully counted and the present Warden, Major J. R. Rose, was kind enough to let me know, at the end of the 1970 breeding season, that there were 10,727 occupied nests that year.

While some British-bred black-headed gulls migrate southwards to the Iberian Peninsula and Africa in autumn, others have wandered to Holland and Denmark. But the vast majority of our birds are sedentary, at any rate after the initial dispersal of young birds from their natal colony. In winter the British black-headed gull population is greatly increased by immigrants from the Scandinavian countries and continental Europe east of Belgium, and ringing recoveries show that individual birds return again and again to the same spot. Thus a bird ringed in St James's Park, London, on 18 February 1939, survived the war years flying to and fro across the southern North Sea. After being recovered, or controlled as the technical word goes, in St James's Park on 25 February 1945 it was finally recovered in Denmark in June 1948. The longest-lived black-headed gull seems to have been one ringed in Czechoslovakia on 24 May 1914 and recovered in Prague on 31 March 1939.

Although the food of the black-headed gull consists mainly of animal matter, a great deal of refuse is taken in winter. It is said to consume something approaching its own weight in food every day. An East German ornithologist who analysed the diet of the black-headed gull in one rural area found that they ate 46% earthworms, 20% fish, 14·5% insects and 11·9% mammals.

Black-headed gull colonies have provided a traditional source of eggs for human consumption. In 1650 Sir Thomas Browne mentions cart-loads of black-headed gulls' eggs being sent to Norwich from the Broads. As late as 1949 a Cambridge poulterer was handling upwards of 1,000 eggs weekly in the breeding season and selling them at 6d each. In former times the young gulls were also taken for food. The famous colony at Norbury in Staffordshire is said to have provided up to fifty dozen young gulls, just out of the nest, during a single morning's trapping.

Gulls are great bathers. First this black-headed gull lowers its body into the water while the wings are partly spread above the surface. The head, almost submerged, is shaken to and fro (left). Then, the head and body are raised, apparently by altering their buoyancy, and the wings in their turn are lowered into the water and shaken so vigorously that, in the illustration below, many of the feathers are blurred even though the exposure was a mere 1/1000 sec. This bird, which was photographed in July at a Yorkshire breeding colony, still has the dark chocolate-brown facial mask of the summer plumage.

14

Feeding habits of the black-headed gull (1): on a sewage farm. Black-headed gulls are perhaps the commonest and most characteristic of all sewage-farm birds. In some areas a quite specialised feeding method is in use to pick edible scraps off the surface of sludge-tanks. The gulls fly low against the wind, swoop down over the surface, hover momentarily while almost touching down with their feet, and seize the desired morsel in their bills. Thus floating fragments of edible matter are obtained without the bird having to settle in a liquid which might prove damaging to its plumage or even cause its death (opposite).

16

Feeding habits of the black-headed gull (2): by the shore. Here all kinds of feeding techniques are used and often a concentration of suitable food will attract a concentration of birds. At Seahouses, Northumberland, in September 1970, I came across a big gathering of black-headed gulls feeding close inshore. They were swimming to and fro in the water just beyond the breaking waves, eagerly searching for and gobbling up the many insects and crustaceans that had been flooded out of mats of dried seaweed by an advancing and unusually high tide (left). These birds had learnt to avoid the breaking waves by flying a few feet up in the air just as a wave passed, and then dropping down to the water again to continue feeding (below).

Feeding habits of the black-headed gull (3): foot-paddling. This behaviour is found in all gulls and in many other species of bird. Here a black-headed gull, photographed in August when it had lost almost all the black head of its summer plumage, is foot-paddling on the shore. It moves its feet rapidly up and down, shifting its weight meanwhile from one leg to the other, in very shallow water, moving slowly backwards and looking intently downwards. Every now and then it snatches up a morsel of food—a small worm or crustacean, which has been disturbed by the churning up of the mud. This particular bird foot-paddled in water only, and is shown here as it reached the end of its 'beat', that is, the edge of the pool it was feeding in. A moment later it would settle again in the centre of the pool and repeat its backward movement towards the edge.

Feeding habits of the black-headed gull (4) : in towns. Illustrated here is a typical urban population of black-headed gulls in winter. A flock of some 50–70 birds establishes itself every winter in the Queen's Gardens, in the centre of Hull, feeding on scraps thrown by visitors. It is only in the last 100 years that black-headed gulls have taken to wintering in large towns. In December 1870 the appearance of the first black-headed gull on the river Spree in Berlin was an unusual enough event to merit publication, and it was not until the winter of 1894-5 that black-headed gulls appeared in numbers in central London. Many thousands of these gulls now winter in Europe's towns, feeding entirely on food provided, directly or indirectly, by man.

Typical winter gull habitat: a refuse tip. These birds are momentarily resting on the rough gravel track round the perimeter of the tip. Besides two great black-backed gulls there are several herring gulls and, as usual in such places, many black-headed gulls. Three of these last, on the left, are drinking from puddles. Refuse tips have probably played a vital role in promoting the increase in numbers of gulls during the present century. This one, at Beverley, Yorkshire, supports several hundred gulls throughout the year, the birds roosting in some grassy fields nearby.

20

Black-headed gull behaviour (1): the so-called Forward display, expressive at times of aggression, but at other times of attachment, is performed here by a bird swimming near its nest in a Yorkshire breeding colony in May. The behaviour of the black-headed gull formed the subject of a pioneering study by F. B. Kirkman, published in 1937 under the title *Bird behaviour*. Since then it has perhaps been more intensively studied than the behaviour of any other bird, with the possible exception of the herring gull.

Black-headed gull behaviour (2): a variant of the Forward display. This bird, which has a tiny feather from recent preening adhering to its lower mandible, is calling plaintively while moving its head up and down with the wings somewhat extended and the body depressed.

The Lesser Black-backed Gull *Larus fuscus*

The more slender and shorter bill, dark grey rather than black mantle, and smaller size, are usually better characters with which to distinguish this species from the great black-backed gull than leg colour, for in winter the legs of both species tend to be more or less whitish. The lesser black-back is another gull which has extended its breeding range during this century, to Iceland, Denmark and the Netherlands, for example. In England it has mostly been confined to the northern and more particularly the north-western counties, though occasional pairs have nested in the south, the Midlands and East Anglia since the war. Recently, about 100 pairs have bred on Orfordness in Suffolk. In Scotland and Ireland the lesser black-backed gull is widespread.

The breeding biology of the lesser black-backed

gull has been studied at Walney Island and on Skomer. The birds arrive in March and lay their eggs in May. Average clutch size is about 2·7 and between one and two chicks are raised per pair. Most of the eggs that fail to hatch are eaten by lesser black-backed gulls! The nests are normally on fairly flat ground in dunes, on cliff slopes and cliff tops, and on the open moorland, but one on the Bristol Channel island of Steepholme was three feet above ground in a privet bush, and the species has nested on the roofs of houses and warehouses in South Wales.

Although lesser black-backed gulls normally breed in mixed colonies with herring gulls, interbreeding is very rare. The nests and eggs of the two species cannot be separately identified and even the young are difficult to tell apart. One such mixed colony was started on the Lancashire fells in the 1930's and now numbers thousands of pairs of gulls. The nests are scattered over several miles of wild and uneven fell, made up of heathery knolls, peaty hollows and gullies, and patches of stone and rock. As soon as they have hatched, the young gulls crouch and hide in the heather and whortleberries. In 1970 counts in two different parts of the colony gave 12% and 31% herring gulls.

Little quantitative information is available about the food of the lesser black-backed gull. Fifty-five Pembrokeshire birds contained relatively little: sixteen had beetle remains, seven had grass, sixteen had fish remains, six contained earth and eight contained vegetable matter. Another investigation showed that fish and marine organisms comprised over half the food taken. The lesser black-backed gull has been watched plunging into the water from a height of 8–10 feet in order to take eels. The birds never submerge and, when successful, they invariably take the eel and settle on the nearest piece of dry land to devour it.

Up to 1969, 61,814 lesser black-backed gulls had been ringed in the British Isles and 2,607 recovered. British-bred birds migrate southwestwards at the end of the summer, reaching the Bay of Biscay in August, the Iberian Peninsula in September and North Africa a little later. By October some have travelled as far as the Canary Isles, Sardinia and Sicily. A very few eccentric birds have moved from England to Scandinavia or even Iceland. Up to 1968, only 30 foreign-ringed birds had been recovered in Britain: most of these came from Norway, Sweden and the Faeroes. The longest-lived British lesser-black-backed gull so far recorded was 15 years old.

Adult lesser black–backed gull in summer plumage, Walney Island, Lancashire, May, 1970. This bird would probably be about 21 inches long and something under 2 lbs in weight. The dark grey mantle serves to distinguish the British from the Scandinavian lesser black-backed gull, which has a slate black mantle. The herring gull's mantle is a much paler shade of grey. The lesser black–backed gull is the only British breeding gull to have yellow legs, but their colour changes during the year from a brilliant deep yellow in March–May to whitish, with varying degrees of yellowish tint, in winter.

Adult lesser black-backed gull in winter plumage, photographed on a refuse tip near York in September. All four large *Larus* gulls, the common, herring, lesser and great black-backed, have their heads, necks and upper breasts more or less streaked with brown in winter and the lesser black-backed is more heavily streaked than any of the others. Whereas, up till the 1940's, it was only occasionally recorded in winter, an increasing number of birds seem now to be overwintering here, especially in western and south-western Britain. It is not in general a very common refuse-tip feeder.

28

Courtship behaviour of the lesser black-backed gull: one bird of a pair leans forward and pecks vigorously at the grass. This is an action which, at other times and between individuals of different pairs, signifies aggression.

Courtship behaviour of the lesser black-backed gull:
the female of a pair approaches the male while
making a series of tossing movements with her head
and uttering a begging call. This head-tossing is the
normal preliminary to courtship feeding and copulation.

A group of breeding lesser black-backed gulls at Walney Island, Lancashire. Taken from a fixed hide, this photograph shows the birds completely relaxed. At least four of them are incubating, for this photograph was taken in May when all the nests had eggs. The mate of the sitting bird usually stands on guard near the nest. It was this Walney Island colony of lesser black-backed and herring gulls which figured in the film and book called *Signals for Survival* by the Oxford based Dutch ornithologist Professor Niko Tinbergen. Since the first lesser black-backed gull's nest was found here in 1926 these birds have increased astonishingly. After ten years there were over 200 pairs and, by 1956, there were probably 5,000 pairs of lesser black-backed gulls and an equal number of herring gulls.

Among the thousands of normal lesser black–backed gulls at Walney Island a few aberrant birds have conspicuous white patches on the upperside of their wings. In 1962 four birds with these white patches were noticed on Skomer Island, and similar birds have been observed in Holland and Iceland. One such is seen here at Walney Island flying with a normal bird to which it was possibly mated. In recent years this rapidly expanding colony has spread from stable grassy dunes to the surrounding beaches, roadsides and even to the gravel workings seen here in the background.

An unusual clutch of lesser black–backed gull's eggs. Two are pale blue and almost unspotted; the third is normal. The nest–site, in an old box on the open beach, is also unusual for the species, but at Walney Island, where this photograph was taken, large numbers of lesser black–backed gulls nest on the beaches. Note how the nest-cup is levelled by the placing of most of the nest-material on the lower (left) side.

The Herring Gull *Larus argentatus*

The herring gull is, of course, the familiar seagull of our shores and seaside resorts, where its loud and melodious call is heard throughout the year, often from birds circling and soaring overhead. It is the gull which normally follows ships and accompanies the fishing boats back from the fishing grounds. Whether or not it is in fact a relatively recent colonist in Europe from the New World, this bird has certainly carved a permanent niche for itself in the literature and the landscape of England and the other North Sea countries.

Not nearly enough accurate information is available to assess the population dynamics of the herring gull in the British Isles. All one can say with certainty is that numbers have increased rapidly during this century. According to one authority they may have

c

doubled in the last twenty years and he concluded that the British herring gull population may be increasing at a rate of 10% per annum. But these suggestions are based on flimsy evidence. At some colonies the increase has been very striking. Take, for example, the colony on the Isle of May. The first pair of herring gulls nested there in 1907; there were 455 pairs by 1936; 3,000 in 1954, and the estimate for 1967 was 11,000 pairs.

Homing experiments in Germany have demonstrated the herring gull's navigational ability. Of Memmert birds released at a distance from their home, 84% returned to the breeding colony: one did the 450 km. journey from Berlin in four days. Ringing recoveries have shown that herring gulls can live for up to 17, 26, 28 or even 31 years in the wild. Captive birds have lived for 41, 44 and even 49 years, and in the nineteenth century a bird on the Faeroes lived for a record 64 years, returning every winter to a farm house where it had been reared.

The herring gull's diet is extremely varied, including fish, molluscs, earthworms, insects and corn. In North Wales individual herring gulls have been found to have eaten the placenta of a cow, six feet of sheep's intestine, and two tomato sandwiches in a polythene bag! Morris's *British Birds* has an entertaining account of a tame herring gull which fed largely on sparrows which it caught in its owner's garden and swallowed whole.

In some colonies at least herring gulls have been shown to raise fewer than one young bird per pair each year. In one colony every 100 eggs laid only yielded 25 fully fledged gulls. The herring gull does not breed until it is four or five years old. The average annual mortality of adults is thought to be around 10%.

Although in some countries, and perhaps especially among sea-faring folk, the herring gull has always been much loved, its predatory habits in the breeding season and its rapid increase in numbers have combined to make it the target of numerous attempts at control. In this country, for example, the first published description of a new nature reserve at Bempton in Yorkshire, newly acquired by the Royal Society for the Protection of Birds, contained a broad hint that control measures against the breeding herring gulls would speedily be undertaken. In the Netherlands, from 1954 onwards, a campaign of control has been in force apparently aimed at maintaining breeding numbers of herring gulls at or below 10,000 pairs in the country as a whole, and at keeping certain important reserves, including, for example, the entire island of Vlieland, completely free of breeding herring gulls. Thus a governmental department fixes the number of breeding herring gulls there are to be in the Netherlands, as well as their distribution. Similarly, in this country two government departments, the Ministry of Agriculture and the Nature Conservancy, have been responsible for experiments in herring gull control and for various schemes of control both inside and outside nature reserves, though little or no information on this work has been made available to the public.

Herring gull plumage (1): winter. The heads and necks of these two birds, photographed in December in their breeding colony in the Yorkshire fishing port of Whitby, are heavily streaked with grey-brown. Some fifty pairs of herring gulls now nest here on the roofs of houses and on chimney stacks. It is clear that, at any rate at Whitby, some birds remain mated, and in the breeding colony, throughout the year.

Herring gull plumage (2): summer. This mated pair of herring gulls was photographed at Flamborough, Yorkshire, in May. The male, slightly larger, stands behind the female on the rounded clay cliff-top. Before its plumage is fully adult the immature herring gull undergoes at least six moults, three complete and three partial, involving a series of plumage changes from streaky brown all over to white, silver-grey and black.

The head of an incubating herring gull appears above the bluebells and red campions which surround its nest on Skomer Island, Pembroke-shire. This bird was photographed on a hot sunny afternoon in May and it is interesting to note that there is water dropping from the tip of its bill. I have seen the bills of both herring and great black-backed gulls dripping water steadily in this way on a hot day.

Typical winter gull habitat: a fish dock. In this photograph, taken at Hull, Yorkshire, the central position is occupied by a great black-backed gull, one of the world's largest species, while half-a-dozen herring gulls around it grab what they can. The great black-backed gull, in particular, has been very successful in exploiting refuse available at fish docks like Hull and Milford Haven and flocks of 100 or more are commonplace at such places.

Each of the herring gull's calls is associated with a different posture or situation. Here, a bird on a Lincolnshire refuse-tip in February is uttering the so-called Mew Call, more often heard in the breeding colony. The head is stretched forward and downwards so that the neck is arched in a characteristic manner, and the wings are held very slightly away from the body. The call itself, as its name implies, is a long drawn-out wailing note. The German ornithologist Goethe, an expert on the herring gull and author of a book on the subject, listed thirteen different calls, tried to explain the function or meaning of each, and even rendered them into musical notation.

Among herring gulls in particular cannibalism is by no means rare, though there is no means of knowing whether the herring gull on the left in this photograph taken at Walney Island, Lancashire, is carrying away a herring or lesser black–backed gull chick. It seems to be only a few gulls in each colony which develop the habit of flying about the colony and swooping on any unguarded chick they see. The smaller ones are swallowed whole. Other chicks are killed by being pecked by neighbouring adults into whose territories they unwittingly trespass. The structure seen here in the background is a hide.

A pair of herring gulls nest-building. The male collects a large bundle of grass in his beak and then takes it to the female, who sits in the half-finished nest as if incubating. From time to time she moves round while still in the nest, pulling the nest material inwards, towards her, with her bill. The finished nest is a rather flat, untidy structure with a large but shallow cup, usually more substantially built than that of the lesser black-backed gull.

The chick is about to emerge from this herring gull's egg at Walney Island, Lancashire. It has already chipped a hole approximately in the centre of the upper surface of the egg. This much enlarged photograph shows well the egg tooth, a hard knob-like appendage on the tip of the chick's bill which enables it to break through the egg-shell. Herring gull's eggs vary a great deal in colour, but most are olive-green, heavily blotched with black-brown. The incubation period of the herring gull is 27 days and three is the normal clutch size.

The Great Black-backed Gull *Larus marinus*

The breeding range of the great black-backed gull in the British Isles extends round the coasts of Scotland, Wales and Ireland and western England, and inland in Lancashire and northern Scotland. It is perhaps commonest in the Orkneys and the Hebrides. It does not breed at all on the east coast of England. Migratory movements are apparently not undertaken by British birds, but there is a large-scale movement of Scandinavian and Russian-bred birds in autumn down the east coast of Britain, and many of these probably remain here through the winter. Investigations conducted by the British Trust for Ornithology have suggested that there were about 1,800 breeding pairs of great black-backed gulls in England and Wales only in 1956 and about 7,000 wintering birds in 1963. It has certainly increased in numbers during this century and become much more common inland, especially on refuse tips, where in the 1930's it was in most areas rare or unknown.

The great black-backed gull has the reputation of being the most voracious and predatory of all our gulls. One is said to have swallowed eleven herrings at a single sitting. On Skomer these gulls feed on birds: manx shearwaters, puffins and kittiwakes are taken in quantity, not to mention numerous young herring and lesser black-backed gulls. Some great black-backs even make a speciality of preying on adult gulls of the two smaller species. On Skomer, too, rabbits form an important part of the great black-back's diet. One shot on Skomer disgorged a full-grown rabbit, completely intact, which must have been swallowed whole. Apart from feeding commonly on refuse tips inland, the great black-back may be seen feeding in fields and even following the plough.

In its breeding biology the great black-backed gull does not differ significantly from the herring and lesser black-backed gulls, though it more often nests in single pairs or very small, scattered colonies. Many of the larger colonies of the smaller species of gull have a few pairs of great black-backs.

Like other gulls, the great black-back has two moults each year. Between January and March the body feathers only are moulted; between June and November all the feathers, including those of the wings and tail, are moulted. The moult of the great black-back's primary, or flight, feathers, is extremely regular, starting with the first, or innermost, primary and continuing in sequence to the tenth or outermost, the moult being exactly synchronised in each wing. This ensures that, at any one time, there are only two incompletely grown feathers in each wing, and the two wings continue to 'match' each other throughout the process, which takes six or seven months to complete. The twenty-four secondary wing-feathers of the great black-backed gull are moulted in two sequences, the first starting with the innermost feather and progressing outwards, the second beginning with the outermost feather and progressing inwards. Thus the gull replaces all its feathers without its powers of flight being adversely affected. The feathers of the tail are moulted in a more haphazard manner.

Walney Island, Lancashire, 21 June 1970. When very small, the baby great black-backed gull hides by crouching in a crevice or in vegetation. Later, it runs fast and strongly and, if chased, will turn and peck at a hand outstretched towards it. Its legs are very well developed from early on and so is the bill. Indeed, this brawny, long-legged little creature with its shaggy speckled down is already quite formidable when only a week or two old. Although great black-backed and other gull chicks appear to roam at will, in fact they remain in a well-defined territory, which is defended by their parents.

The immature great black-backed gull is not very dissimilar from immature herring and lesser black-backed gulls, but it is usually whiter about the head and breast and darker on the back, so that it tends to be more contrasty. Its larger size is not very noticeable, but the long, heavy bill may serve to identify it. This particular bird, in its first winter, was photographed on a Yorkshire refuse tip.

The great black-backed gull is normally exceedingly shy. Indeed, it is much harder to photograph at the nest than the other gulls. But in winter, on the fish dock, it becomes bold and aggressive, and will even approach to within a few feet of men at work to grab and gobble up any piece of fish offal they drop or throw away. This photograph was taken at Hull in early March and the bird figured in it has almost lost its winter plumage streaks on the head which are in any case not very conspicuous in this species.

52

One of the common behavioural postures found in all gulls is the so-called Hunched, which this adult great black-backed gull is shown here adopting on a Yorkshire refuse tip. It is rather similar to the Forward (see p.21 above) but the bird's head is withdrawn and the back is more hunched. It is thought normally to represent submission.

The Long Call, shown here, is the best known of all gull calls, probably because of its loudness. In the great black-backed gull it consists of a series of disyllabic notes which could be rendered oo-er oo-er oo-er, uttered, as seen here, with the neck extended upwards and forwards. These very loud notes are usually preceded by a series of short gruff calls with the head bent forwards and downwards so that it is almost between the bird's legs. This particular bird is in its third or fourth winter, that is to say, it is a sub-adult. It has a black bar on the bill and some brownish feathers on its mantle and wing.

53

Skomer Island, Pembrokeshire, a National Nature Reserve which has been mentioned several times in this book, supports a numerous population of breeding gulls of four different species, with up to 200 pairs of great black-backs. These have been subjected to a sustained programme of control. Every year since 1960 as many adults as possible have been trapped or shot and the eggs punctured to stop them hatching. In this period over 1,000 adult great black-backed gulls have been eliminated, but the breeding population has only been reduced from about 260 pairs to about 170 pairs. The aim of this destruction is to increase the numbers of other breeding sea-birds, on which the great black-backs prey. In this photograph the incubating bird of a pair of great black-backed gulls is visible on the right, while its mate stands 'guard' on the extreme left. In the distance is the Pembrokeshire mainland.

Some of the Skomer great black-backed gulls nest on grassy slopes above the cliffs, laying their eggs among clumps of thrift of varying shades of pink.

Every autumn large numbers of great black-backed gulls pass down the east coast on migration. Those shown here, accompanied by a solitary oystercatcher and a young herring gull (extreme left), formed part of a large flock which had been resting on the extensive sands at the mouth of the Wash. Careful scrutiny of the photograph shows that many of them are moulting their flight-feathers. Holme-next-the-Sea, 12 September 1971.

The Common Gull *Larus canus*

One of those birds, like the Sandwich tern, with a
ridiculous English name, the common gull is in fact
the rarest of the six British breeding gulls. At least,
up till 1969, fewer common gulls had been ringed
than any of the other five species. The actual figures,
giving the total number of each species ringed up to
1969, are as follows: black-headed gull–113,651;
herring gull–99,718; lesser black-backed gull–
61,814; kittiwake–31,053; great black backed gull–
8,381; common gull–7,861.

The common gull is not always easy to distinguish
from the herring gull, but it is appreciably smaller
and has a more slender and shorter bill. Also, the
mantle is a slightly darker grey and the legs are
greenish rather than flesh-coloured as in the herring
gull.

In Europe as a whole, as opposed to Britain and Ireland, common gull numbers have increased rapidly during this century and the bird has considerably extended its range. The first recorded nesting in Holland was in 1908; by 1962 there were 660 breeding pairs in twenty-six different colonies. Since 1955 the common gull has nested in Iceland. In 1966 there was a remarkable extension of its range southwards: it nested on Lake Neuchâtel in Switzerland and on the French, or southern, shore of Lake Geneva. In Britain there is little evidence of an increase in numbers apart from the recent colonisation of south-west Scotland. In England it is rare indeed. There is a steadily dwindling colony at Dungeness and a few pairs have bred in Anglesey since 1963, as well as in eastern England since 1965. But in winter the common gull is a widespread and common bird throughout England, and ringing recoveries have shown that most of these birds come from Scandinavia and Germany. The longest-lived common gull so far recorded? Perhaps the one ringed as a chick on Heligoland on 21 June 1949 and found dead, oiled, on the beach at Winterton, Norfolk on 23 March 1969.

The food of the common gull has been studied by the Russian ornithologist Belopol'skii, who found that, in the Barents Sea, one quarter was fish, one quarter was insects, and over one third was vegetable matter, mainly berries. Common gulls eat eggs on occasion and are adept at robbing other birds, especially black-headed gulls and lapwings, of their prey.

During the breeding season, common gulls roost in their breeding colony, on or near the nests, though they do not begin to do this until the eggs are laid. In a study of the winter roosting habits of the common gull in the Severn estuary it was found that the main roost was on sand-banks or on the water, according to tide, some ten miles south of Gloucester, near Frampton. The number of common gulls using this roost was thought to reach 25,000 at times. The birds started leaving their roost well before sunrise and it was virtually empty within half an hour of the first birds leaving. They dispersed in all directions but followed well-marked flight lines to their feeding areas, which were up to twenty miles from the roost. About two hours before sunset parties of common gulls flew up from the fields and headed for the roost. Gradually the numbers increased until, as daylight faded, the passage of returning birds was nearly continuous. The authors of this valuable study were struck by the remarkable ability of these gulls to find their way back to the roost even in thick mist or driving rain with low cloud.

This young common gull, with its underparts illuminated by the light reflected from snow on the ground below, is having some difficulty in perching on a tennis-court fence in a town park. It is in its second winter, having acquired a large amount of pure grey on its mantle, and become more or less pure white underneath. The black-tipped bill is typical of young birds while the bird's slender, elegant, shape is characteristic of the common gull.

Shown here together are an adult and an immature common gull in flight over the Humber. This photograph was taken in winter from the ferry, which the common gulls have learnt to follow to and fro across the river in their search for scraps of bread and other refuse thrown overboard. The immature bird, on the left, has brown feathers in its wing as well as grey, and it has a good deal more black towards the end of the wing, with fewer white spots on the wing-tip.

Man-made food sources have been exploited by the common gull just as effectively as by the other species of gull. Indeed, in some towns it is a good deal more abundant than the black-headed gull. In Hull common gulls perch freely on the chimneys and roofs of houses and feed regularly on park lawns and playing fields and even in gardens. Here a flock of common gulls is gathering to pick up a handful of scraps of bread thrown for them onto some snow-covered waste land in that city.

The evident excitement of this pair of common gulls, both mewing loudly, is a product of their arrival back at the nest together after the disturbance caused by my entry into the hide. One of the three eggs is chipped and about to hatch. This nest was part of a small colony on a flat grassy islet on the edge of Loch Lochinvar, Kirkcudbright, and the photograph was taken on 4 June. Note the brilliant white plumage of the head and neck, so different from the streaky brown of the winter plumage.

Nest and nesting habitat of the common gull in south-west Scotland. The bird seen here incubating in a clump of sea-thrift belongs to a small scattered coastal colony near the Ross of Kirkcudbright. The nests are on or near the summits of rock outcrops not far above the high water mark and quite easily accessible. For many people living in England, south-west Scotland is the nearest place to find breeding common gulls.

Wing-stretching, which seems to be particularly frequent among all the gulls, is demonstrated here by a common gull. One wing is stretched outwards, and at the same time the leg is held out sideways and the tail is somewhat fanned. This bird, photographed on 1 November, is in fully adult plumage but the black tip to the bill probably shows that it is in fact a young bird in its third winter. It was photographed on a town playing field, a favourite haunt of this species, which it visits in order to rest and preen on the dry flat ground as well as to hunt for worms under the short grass.

All the six British breeding gulls follow the plough but the common gull perhaps does so more than the others, except possibly the black-headed gull. The birds shown here, all common gulls save for the right-hand bird facing away which is a black-headed gull, have just dropped down behind the passing tractor and are searching eagerly for worms. Photographed in November, they already have the streaky heads of their winter plumage. Young common gulls are, curiously enough, very rare in autumn and winter flocks of this species: there is none present here.

The Kittiwake *Rissa tridactyla*

The kittiwake gets its English name from its most frequent call, which is repeated over and over again in the nesting colonies. On Lundy Island the birds were thought to be saying Keep awake! Keep awake! Readily identified by its wholly black wing-tips lacking the white spots of the other gulls, its short, slightly forked tail, greenish bill and black legs and feet, the adult kittiwake is only sixteen inches long and weighs under a pound. Quite apart from the black markings on their head, neck and tail, the young birds can easily be distinguished in flight by the conspicuous diagonal black bar on their wings.

The kittiwake is distributed right round the Pole north of about 47° North to within the Arctic Circle. The most southerly breeding stations of the Atlantic subspecies are in Brittany and Newfoundland. There is only one other member of the genus *Rissa*, the red-legged kittiwake of the North Pacific.

The kittiwake is thought to have been increasing in numbers in Britain during the present century, though some colonies, such as those on the Isle of May and Lundy Island, have decreased in numbers. But others have expanded, often in spectacular fashion. Thus at Scarborough a single pair nested on the cliff below the castle in 1940 but there were 280 pairs in 1956 and about 650 in 1966. Kittiwakes leave their breeding colonies in July-September and young birds may be seen in the centre of the North Sea by early August. In winter kittiwakes are widely distributed throughout the North Atlantic. The return to the nesting colonies begins in February.

Some idea of the way first-year kittiwakes disperse from their natal colony is given by records of seventeen birds, all ringed as nestlings on the Farne Islands in June or July 1959 and recovered in 1960 in the following countries: England (2), Belgium (1), Netherlands (2), Denmark (1), Germany (3), France (1), Morocco (1), Ireland (1), Newfoundland (2) and Greenland (3).

The kittiwake's nest-building is a communal activity, flocks of fifty or more birds flying inland to pull out grass by the roots or collect water-weed or mud from a pond. The nest itself is more elaborate than that of most other gulls and many nests survive intact from one year to the next. According to the Russian ornithologist Belopol'skii, a kittiwake's nest weighs about three kilograms. He estimated that the kittiwakes nesting on the Kharlov Islands in the

Barents Sea use about eighteen tons of nest material each year. The kittiwake lays in May and early June and young may be seen on the wing from about 10 July. It feeds to a large extent on small fish which are often caught by means of a very shallow dive or plunge from a height of about twenty feet.

According to Pennant, a certain gentleman ate six kittiwakes on one occasion before dinner, but the kittiwake has not been persecuted for food so much as for its feathers, which were used for women's hats in the nineteenth century. Even after the Seabirds Protection Act of 1869 made it illegal to shoot them in the breeding season, the slaughter continued after 1 August. The kittiwake has few natural enemies, though it is sometimes driven off its nesting ledge and even its nest by guillemots.

This group of resting kittiwakes, which includes one oiled bird on the right, was photographed on the Yorkshire coast on 19 September 1968. Already, these birds are in the distinctive winter plumage, which is acquired in August and September and retained until February or March. It is identical to the summer plumage except for a large and very conspicuous black spot, with smudged edges, some distance behind the eye; a smoky-grey patch on the nape, rather indistinct and variable; and varying amounts of blackish immediately around the eye.

Kittiwake colonies normal and abnormal (1): a typical kittiwake colony on chalk cliffs, Flamborough Head, Yorkshire. In this photograph the birds are still incubating. A few weeks later, the ledges will be crowded with young birds as well as adults. These nests are part of England's largest kittiwake colony, which stretches for nine miles along the cliffs from Flamborough to Speeton. So far it seems to have defied accurate counting: figures published in recent years, some of them optimistically exact, have given the number of nests as follows– 1952: 17,000; 1957: 22,100; 1964: 31,195; and 1967: 19,000.

Kittiwake colonies normal and abnormal (2): Here, on a building at Lowestoft harbour, Suffolk, the kittiwakes' nests are packed close together along a single, very narrow, sloping ledge. In spite of frequent losses of nests in windy weather, numbers here increased rapidly from two pairs in 1958 to thirty-five in 1970. Until recently this was the only kittiwake colony between Flamborough Head and the Isle of Purbeck in Dorset, but kittiwakes have recently colonised the Isle of Wight and seem about to breed on the power station at Dungeness.

Kittiwake colonies normal and abnormal: (3) Nearly every window-ledge on this Tyneside warehouse, at North Shields, almost two miles from the sea, is now occupied by one or more pairs of nesting kitti-wakes. This unusual colony, which was established in 1949 by four pairs of birds, has been intensively studied: it is one of the few in this country where the nests are easily accessible so that birds can be ringed and watched at close quarters. However, there is a breeding colony of kittiwakes on the nearly flat boulder-strewn island of Tyvholm in the northern Kattegat, and occasional pairs of kittiwakes have nested on the flat beaches of Norfolk.

Kittiwakes make regular overland flights, though usually for short distances only, in search of nest material and in order to drink. These birds were photographed at a small cliff-top pond near Bempton, Yorkshire, in July. They arrive in straggling groups of up to fifty or a hundred birds and often submerge their heads and necks entirely as they plunge down into the water. A quick gulp or two of fresh water and they are off again, bathing being usually carried out in the sea.

In common with other gulls, the kittiwake regurgitates food for its chicks. Feeding is initiated when, after pointing its bill upwards and calling shrilly, the hungry nestling begins to peck at the adult's bill. The adult then opens its bill, pointing it downwards, and the chick takes the food from inside its vermilion-coloured throat. The young kittiwake in down is quite unlike the cryptically-coloured chicks of the other gulls. It has a whiteish head and underparts and a plain unspotted grey-brown back.

Taken at Skomer Island, Pembrokeshire, this photograph shows two neighbouring pairs of kittiwakes copulating on their nests. In the kittiwake, the female remains seated during copulation. The male, while mounting her, flaps his wings occasionally to keep balance and points his head and bill downward towards his mate, who may turn her head towards him. The droppings show up a brilliant white against the black basalt rock of Skomer.

These nearly full-grown kittiwake nestlings will soon be flying. Blackish eyes, head spots and very prominent black neck-bars distinguish them from the adults. Note too, their black bills and black-tipped tails. Bempton, Yorkshire, 19 July 1970. The usual kittiwake clutch is two or three. One or other adult normally remains continuously at the nest until the young birds are ready to fly.

Like all gulls, kittiwakes will fight on occasion, especially in territorial disputes. Here one bird has seized another just above its bill and will not let go its grip. The result: both birds go spiralling downwards towards the sea, locked in combat. Sometimes, when this happens, they separate in mid-air, sometimes they splash into the water still fighting.

Sometimes kittiwakes posture aggressively at one another outside the breeding season. These two were photographed in September in winter plumage.

The Less Common British Gulls

Besides the six common British gulls so far described, there are a further twelve species which many would regard as more or less rare. These fall into several well-defined categories. There is, in the first place, a group of wanderers from the New World, which occasionally cross the Atlantic Ocean. Commonest of these exceptional rarities which, curiously enough, are all 'black-headed' in type, is Bonaparte's gull, *Larus philadelphia,* which has been recorded here on at least twenty-two occasions. Unusual among gulls in that it nests up to twenty feet up in spruce or other trees in Canada's northern coniferous zone, it is not unlike our black-headed gull, but has a slate-black, not chocolate-brown, head. In the laughing gull, *Larus atricilla,* the entire head is deep black in summer except for the white round the eye which is typical of most of the 'black-headed' gulls. In spite of a definite French record in 1877, British ornithologists have been loth to accept the laughing gull on their list. English records in 1923 and 1957 were turned down, but the laughing gull was identified in Sweden in 1964 and in France again in 1965, and so at last, the 1966 Kentish bird achieved acceptance for this species on the British List. Needless to say, its call is described in the literature as a ha-ha-ha-ha-ha. The third American species is Franklin's gull, *Larus pipixcan*, which was identified in Hampshire in the spring of 1970, far away from its usual winter quarters in the Gulf of Mexico and along the Pacific coast of South America. A long way, too, from its summer quarters in the Canadian prairies. It is the only gull which migrates regularly across the equator.

Three others of the twelve rarer British gulls are vagrants from southern Eurasia. The slender-billed gull, *Larus genei*, which breeds extremely sparsely in the western Mediterranean but in large concentrations in the Black Sea, has been identified twice in Sussex, in 1960 and 1963. The great black-headed gull, *Larus ichthyaetus*, also breeds in the Black Sea, but no further west. It has been recorded on some half-dozen occasions in Britain. The Mediterranean gull, *Larus melanocephalus*, is a curiosity, and very much a bird to look out for, since it has been extending its range recently, starting to breed since 1930 in Hungary, East Germany and Holland. In 1968 a pair nested successfully in a Hampshire black-headed gull colony. Since the war, there have been over 400 records of this species in Britain.

Forming a group on its own, so to speak, is the little gull, *Larus minutus*, the world's smallest gull, which is probably now the commonest of our twelve rarer gulls. In recent years it has occurred in increasing numbers on passage, especially in the autumn. On the coast of Fife and Angus it is now present throughout the year, with peaks of over 300 individuals in the last three years. It has nested in Holland, but not recently. Some breed in Scandinavia, but its stronghold is eastwards across Russia. It is a small, elegant version of the black-headed gull with a similar dark hood but a quite different wing-pattern.

The remaining five species of rarer gull are all of them wanderers from the Arctic. In the case of the glaucous gull, *Larus hyperboreus*, however, the word wanderer is not wholly apposite, for it is in fact an annual though scarce winter visitor to eastern Britain. The very similar Iceland gull, *Larus glaucoides,* is much rarer. It breeds in Greenland and Baffin Island only, not Iceland; whereas the glaucous gull is found throughout Arctic regions, all round the Pole. Sabine's gull, *Larus sabini*, is another circumpolar species which has now been shown to be regular in Britain, even becoming quite common in some years. It was discovered in Greenland in 1818 by Captain Edward Sabine of the Royal Artillery. The two rarest Arctic gulls occuring in Britain are the pure white ivory gull, *Pagophila eburnea*, recorded some eighty times here since the first was shot in 1822, and the rosy-tinted Ross's gull, *Rhodostethia rosea*, which has been identified in Britain on less than a dozen occasions. Few ornithologists have visited its breeding colonies along the lower reaches of some of the larger rivers of north-east Siberia.

Rarer British gulls (a): the little gull. The little gull in its first winter plumage is a striking and distinctive bird. The tail is black-tipped and there is a broad dark bar along the wing which merges with the black tips of the primaries. Besides the black spot behind the eye, there are dark patches on the crown and nape. Little gulls have been seen annually at Hornsea Mere, Yorkshire, in recent years, especially in August and September. They are often to be found perched on the posts of a fence which encloses a shallow hard-bottomed area of water where cattle can drink. This bird, photographed at this spot in early September, is probably in moult from juvenile to first-winter plumage.

Rarer British gulls (b): the little gull. The world's smallest gull may one day breed in Britain for it has nested in Holland and it does so also in Denmark, Sweden and Finland. Once a rather scarce winter visitor and passage-migrant, it has now become locally common. The bird illustrated here is an adult in winter plumage.

Rarer British gulls (c): the glaucous gull. Every winter a few glaucous gulls are reported in eastern Britain and in some years they are quite common. Figured here at Filey, Yorkshire, is a young bird in streaky brown plumage instead of the adult's pure white. The bill is distinctive, but the best field character is perhaps the complete absence of black on the wings. The nearest breeding colonies of this Arctic species to the British Isles are in Iceland, where it also interbreeds with the herring gull, Bear Island and the Murman coasts of Russia.

Literature

What follows is a list of fifty of the more important books and papers which have been of use to me in the preparation of this book.

1. *The black-headed gull*

Beer, C.G. 1961–6. Incubation and nest-building behaviour of black-headed gulls. Parts I–V. Behaviour 18:62–106, 19:283–304, 21:13–77 and 155–76, 26:189–213.

Kirkman, F.B. 1937. Bird behaviour. London.

Kruuk, H. 1964. Predators and anti-predator behaviour of the black-headed gull. Leiden.

Makatsch, W. 1952. Die Lachmöwe. Leipzig.

Radford, M.C. 1962. British ringing recoveries of the black-headed gull. Bird Study 9:42–55.

Ytreberg, N.J. 1956. Contribution to the breeding

biology of the black-headed gull (*Larus ridibundus*, L.) in Norway. Nest, eggs and incubation. Nytt Magasin for Zoologi 4: 5–106.

2. *The lesser black-backed gull*
Barnes, J.A.G. 1953. The migration of the lesser black-backed gull. British Birds 46: 238–52.
Barnes, J.A.G. 1961. The winter status of the lesser black-backed gull. Bird Study 8: 127–47.
Brown, R.G.B. 1967. Courtship behaviour in the lesser black-backed gull, *Larus fuscus*. Behaviour 29: 122–53.
Harris, M.P. 1962. Migration of the lesser black-backed gull as shown by ringing data. Bird Study 9: 174–82.
Tinbergen, N. and H. Falkus. 1970. Signals for survival. Oxford.

3. *The herring gull*
Drost, R. and others. 1961. Entwicklung und Aufbau einer Population der Silbermöwe. Journal für Ornithologie 102: 404–29.
Goethe, F. 1956. Die Silbermöwe. Wittenberg Lutherstadt.
Harris, M.P. 1964. Recoveries of ringed herring gulls. Bird Study 11: 183–91.
Threlfall, W. 1968. The food of herring gulls in Anglesey and Caernarvonshire. Nature in Wales 11: 67–73.
Tinbergen, N. 1953. The herring gull's world. London.

4. *The great black-backed gull*

Davis, T.A.W. 1958. The breeding distribution of the great black-backed gull in England and Wales in 1956. Bird Study 5: 191–215.

Harris, M.P. 1962. Recoveries of ringed great black-backed gulls. Bird Study 9: 192–7.

Ingolfsson, A. 1970. The moult of remiges and rectrices in great black-backed gulls *Larus marinus* and glaucous gulls *L. hyperboreus* in Iceland. Ibis 112: 83–92.

Saunders, D.R. 1962. The great black-backed gull on Skomer. Nature in Wales 8: 56–66.

Temme, M. 1966. Uber das Verhaltensrepertoire der Mantelmöwe (*Larus marinus* L.) im Winterhalbjahr. Journal für Ornithologie 107: 70–84.

5. *The common gull*

Barth, E.K. 1955. Egg-laying, incubation and hatching of the common gull (*Larus canus* L.) Ibis 97: 222–39.

Braaksma, S. 1964. Het voorkomen van de Stormmeeuw (*Larus canus* L.). Limosa 37: 58–95.

Kantak, F. 1954. Sturmmöwen auf Langenwerder. Wittenberg Lutherstadt.

Onno, S. 1967. Nesting ecology of the common gull. English summary. Ornitologiline kogumik 4: 146–8.

Onno, S. 1968. The span of life of the common gull and the age structure of its population in Estonia. English summary. Communications of the Baltic Commission for the study of bird migration 5: 108–9

Radford, M.C. 1960. Common gull movements shown by ringing returns. Bird Study 7: 81–93.

Vernon, J.D.R. 1969. Spring migration of the common gull in Britain and Ireland. Bird Study 16: 101–7.

Vernon, J.D.R. 1970. Food of the common gull on grassland in autumn and winter. Bird Study 17: 36–8.

Vernon, J.D.R. and T.P. Walsh. 1966. The common gull in the Severn Estuary in relation to feeding areas, roost sites and behaviour. Proceedings of the Bristol Naturalists' Society 31 : 173–84.

Weidmann, U. 1955. Some reproductive activities of the common gull, *Larus canus* L. Ardea 43 : 85–132.

6. *The kittiwake*

Coulson, J.C. 1963. The status of the kittiwake in the British Isles. Bird Study 10 : 147–79.

Coulson, J.C. and E. White. 1956. A study of colonies of the kittiwake *Rissa tridactyla*. Ibis 98 : 63–79.

Coulson, J.C. and E. White. 1958. The effect of age on the breeding biology of the kittiwake *Rissa tridactyla*. Ibis 100 : 40–51.

Coulson, J.C. and E. White. 1958. Observations on the breeding of the kittiwake. Bird Study 5 : 74–83.

Coulson, J.C. and E. White. 1960. The effect of age and density of breeding birds on the time of breeding of the kittiwake *Rissa tridactyla*. Ibis 102 : 71–86.

Cullen, E. 1957. Adaptations in the kittiwake to cliff nesting. Ibis 99 : 275–302.

Paludan, K. 1955. Some behaviour patterns of *Rissa tridactyla*. Videnskabelige Meddelelser fra Dansk Naturhistorisk Forening i Kobenhavn 114: 1–21.

7. *The less common British gulls*
Billet, D.F. and P.J. Grant. 1971. Franklin's gull in Hampshire: a species new to Britain and Ireland. British Birds 64: 310–13.
Buck, W.F.A. and D.W. Taylor. 1967. Laughing gull in Kent: a species new to Britain and Ireland. British Birds 60: 157–9.
Ferguson-Lees, I.J. 1963. Studies of less familiar birds, 123. Glaucous gull. British Birds 56: 263–6.
Taverner, J.H. 1970. Mediterranean gulls nesting in Hampshire. British Birds 63: 67–79.
Wallace, D.I.M. 1964. Studies of less familiar birds, 128. Slender-billed gull. British Birds 57: 242–7.

Works dealing with more than one species
Belopol'skii, L.O. 1961. Ecology of sea colony birds of the Barents Sea. Jerusalem, Israel. Program for Scientific Translations.
Brown, R.G.B. 1967. Breeding success and population growth in a colony of herring and lesser black-backed gulls *Larus argentatus* and L. *fuscus*. Ibis 109: 502–15.
Dwight, J. 1925. The gulls (Laridae) of the world: their plumages, moults, variations, relationships and distribution. Bulletin of the American Museum of Natural History 52: 63–408.
Harris, M.P. 1964. Aspects of the breeding biology of the gulls *Larus argentatus, L. fuscus* and *L. marinus*. Ibis 106: 432–56.
Harris, M.P. 1965. The food of some *Larus* gulls. Ibis 107: 43–53.

Tinbergen, N. 1960. Comparative studies of the behaviour of gulls (Laridae). A progress report. Behaviour 15:1–70.

Vernon, J.D.R. 1970. Feeding habits and food of the black-headed and common gull. Bird Study 17: 287–96.

A note on the photographs

All the photographs in this book were taken with a 35mm. miniature camera, either a Nikon F or a Nikkormat FT, on Ilford film, FP(3)4 or HP(3)4 according to the light. The exposure was almost never longer than 1/250 sec.; the aperture in no case wider than f.8. Development was in Ilford Hyfin for FP(3)4 and Ilford Microphen for HP(3)4.

Rather more than half of these photographs were taken from a small portable hide made of calico with sleeves for the lenses. This was employed both to photograph breeding gulls at the nest, for example the lesser black-backed gulls and common gulls, and feeding gulls on the shore or on refuse tips. The distance from the camera to the bird varied between a few feet, in the case of close-ups from the hide, to about thirty yards with the longest telephoto lens.

Lenses of five different focal lengths, between 50 and 1,000 mm., were employed for these illustrations. The 300mm. lens was used more than any other, both with and without a hide, but a good number of photographs were taken with the 1,000mm. Reflex Nikkor mirror lens mounted on a heavy tripod. This lens, too, was sometimes used in a hide, as for the bathing and displaying black-headed gulls, and sometimes without, as with the common gull wing-stretching. These fifty-four photographs have been selected from hundreds taken during the last two years in Norfolk, Lincolnshire, Yorkshire, Northumberland, Lancashire and Kirkcudbright. None of them has been reproduced elsewhere.

Index